Lookaftering

poems by

Ray Holmes

Finishing Line Press
Georgetown, Kentucky

Lookaftering

Copyright © 2020 by Ray Holmes
ISBN 978-1-64662-191-0 First Edition
All rights reserved under International and Pan-American Copyright Conventions. No part of this book may be reproduced in any manner whatsoever without written permission from the publisher, except in the case of brief quotations embodied in critical articles and reviews.

ACKNOWLEDGMENTS

Kind thanks to the editors of the following publications, who got early versions of these poems out of the house:

Architrave Press: "Rising Action"
Bad Shoe: "Lookaftering"
Chariton Review: "Traces"
Dialogist: "Black Tern"
Fjords: "Coyote *in Adolescentia*"
Lindenwood Review: "Born of Light and Water, Coyote Joins our Pack"
Midwestern Gothic: "Hidden / Sought"
Modern Poetry Quarterly Review: "Year of the Goat"
Thin Air: "In the Park with False Ruins"

Publisher: Leah Maines
Editor: Christen Kincaid
Cover Art: *Rutscape* by Julie Glossenger, Instagram @jglossenger
Author Photo: Ray Holmes
Cover Design: Elizabeth Maines McCleavy

Printed in the USA on acid-free paper.
Order online: www.finishinglinepress.com
also available on amazon.com

Author inquiries and mail orders:
Finishing Line Press
P. O. Box 1626
Georgetown, Kentucky 40324
U. S. A.

Table of Contents

Shenandoah Black Box 1

Trace Decay: Elko, NV 3

Hidden / Sought 4

Dispatches from the Carlin Unconformity ('92-94) 5

Roses in Boise 7

The Neighborhood Watchers 9

Born of Light and Water, Coyote Joins our Pack 10

At the Regal Convenience 11

Weird Diamonds 12

Coyote *in Adolescentia* 13

Dispatch from Here ('99) 14

Me and Coyote's Last Stand 15

Strike a Match, Blacken 16

Poem for A.'s Incisor 17

Rising Action 19

About the Bird 20

On Refraction 21

In the Park with False Ruins 23

Theory of the Wild 24

In the Heaving of a Static Stampede 25

Traces 26

Year of the Goat 27

Black Tern 29

Grip and Hammer 30

No Image 31

Lookaftering 32

*for Sara
and for my family*

Shenandoah Black Box

This is how we lived:
This is where the jambs perched tight:
Where the door caught the frame:
How the gap beneath breathed:
Beyond this the banister unfurled:
These are the floorboards which sagged under foot:
In this room was the drywall punched through:
In this was it patched:
In these ways the windows rattled under furious skies:
Here is where we took our breakfast:
In this way the eggs were fried:
In this manner we communed:
This is how we clasped hands:
The room in which we ate one-handed:
Here is where the silence stood:
This pose the house assumed:
With this noise the furnace awoke:
This machinery of the house was resurrected:
Among these changes did the light move:
By this did the spark arise:
These bricks were licked by the flame:
This is how clearly the attic could be seen through:
How many shards of sky between the charred rafters:
These were some of our neighbors:
In this order they came out to see:
To this degree were they concerned:
This is the time elapsed before the sirens:
These pitches were howled by the local dogs:
Among these are the things we will recover:

Here are the ways we will regenerate:
And grieve:
And commune:
This is how we continue:

Trace Decay: Elko, NV

sutured with spider's thread / a barbed needle / the something
    of my history
spun slowly / in the night's slow revival / 150 empty miles
cast in all directions / something swept under / swept up
    in the torrential years

once I tried to catch you / in emulsion / increments by color
a hair-thin roll of film / the contour of a lens / the body's sudden
    whir into resetting
bound and boxed / filed witnesses / to a crumbling road
the town's collective carotid / a tent set alive / in the palm
    of a living room
a puppy and her lost name / a bowless gift

the memories blur / X's scratched in dirt / mark *the spot*
something that loosens memory's grip / pries apart
    the crosshairs / unspools the dark
once I tried to catch you / to weave this tender web
to catch you / I cannot / now

Hidden / Sought

A boar's head smirked
on the parlor wall, watching me

smash the latch and crawl knob by knob
into your cabinet of frail dishes

its look of tusky shock all but shouting
while the china clinked

and I cocked my head, ducking like a beetle caught
on its back. I hoped to clink along after a time

with the summer ease of shucking grass
from between my Indian-style legs. By then I figured

what skin would do after years
in the cabinet-blackness, all pillbugged and thin.

What I'm saying, in my own simple terms, is
I knew you would come to dig me out. Knew

that boar was no friend, that shiver in the cabinet
would not be mistaken. I read the bull pines

outside, their jilted needles, and knew
it would come to this:

Set yourself down outside of my keyhole. This
is the only way it could happen.

Dispatches from the Carlin Unconformity ('92-94)

Chipped sawtooth and nail, hammer's bill redheaded in rust,
my mother's hard whomp pins to the wall an icon
her boyfriend cut from a ragged hunk of wood
after hours in the dank of his basement workshop. In truth,

she tacks its hot stare to my snakeful belly
—the icon's crosshatch unvarnished, improvised and atilt,
its shape a fiery eye that patrols the room, counting
trampled Busch cans and doling out *shalts* and *shalt nots*
to no one in particular. In truth, my gut is coming down
with a case of ice cream sandwich jimmied from the patio icebox.

...

Street outside rustles up a midday number and Grand's home
-stitched truck rattles into the driveway. Its body
patched in multicolored steels, a soldered mutant
shambling each morning toward the mines outside of town,
Grand at its ears, tapping his stub of a pointer on the wheel.

I count my own fingers, count them straight to ten,
and weave them over my navel like a soft shell, knowing
the difference between *whole* and *holy*.

...

And of the ever-burning eye, what did it impart? To turn my cheek,
sunburnt as it is, to the mines north of town
and their raucous hood of dustlight.

Grand learned to pilot a pickaxe in those pits. He strode into the deep
of the land, tensing his muscles to the heat and grunge in a way
that sent his tattoo dancing—that dark she-wolf flexing seduction
across his pectoral, that ink and scratch and scar
reminder of the boom days. To the towns farther west,

long since salted across the desert, their clamor reborn
in the sniff of this rogue dog or that… To those decrepit townships
and their wooden adits built just tall enough
for men to step inside and work,
to chip away at the desert's heavy cranium and lower by awful degrees
their bodies-now-ghosts, only to emerge broken and smeared
dark with grease and dust, hauling
that dim glint of what they came for.

Roses in Boise

Burst of fire along the tin shed's wall,
tightly curling petals

of flame-tooth, spiny-stem,
planted by their mother to obscure

the copperblack rash growing
like a Martian landscape

the farther out the summer spreads,
blocking where the boys leaned to piss

after digging up snakes from the neighborless miles
or dipping whole-bodied into the river's thready offshoots.

No venom could shuttle them into disaster,
no threat of drowning,

the boys were wild and stern, grown,
serious in the risks they ignored

and how they tamed the day's fierce hours.
From the shed's dark, one boy pulls a hatchet

and thumbs its dull beak with a dare
blooming in his pupils.

The other spits
and counters with a smile.

The blade is sure, the thud unthunderous
in the grass at their knees. They hunch

by the shed, the ground split
where the hatchet keeps hold.

One boy is mute
at the dull end of the handle; the other

is clenched in face and hand
and now in full body,

the curve of his finger a crescent
moon in grass before them.

While he is rushed away,
the other seeps his grip into the dirt,

easy as water, worries a hole
where the finger can begin

its slow waning
into rot and bushroot, feeding the roses,

their quiet burning along
the shed and its rusted memory.

The Neighborhood Watchers

Beyond the tinsel fences
dividing us from the solid world
a familiar roar brings another week's dairy
from behind the craggy hills. Refrigerated trucks
beating the distance between small towns

into a feverish dust. When they stop at the corner,
we empty our wallets, step into the sunstare,
and glance like escapees at the horizon.

We've heard the nightly yipping, drawing our faces
to those cool windows not tinted by grit. By morning,
three or so rabbits spilled outside the perimeter
and marks from digging in.

At dusk I see shadows hunched on top of the boulders.
Frozen groceries in hand, I make it to my yard
and the outdoor freezer, those figures on the hill just dark
as a quart of vanilla bean melts in my hands.

Born of Light and Water, Coyote Joins our Pack

From high-hung planters,
from a drooped leaf,
you came into our house.
Those first days you cried
like a near-split bulb.
We tried everything,
tucked you into cool soil
until, finally, no sound.

By hands you grew from your cradle,
took count of those with water.
I remember one evening
breaking you loose and running,
dirt all up my arms. I remember
how the plan took shape that morning
and how, careful bloom,
it went off so nicely. It was
what we wanted. That light,
that never-clear
of the neighborhood after hours.

At the Regal Convenience

A swarthy Christ watched me
worry coins in my pocket
like they were halos-to-be-straightened,
humming *Thou shalt not twist*
the profiles of the dead
from his keen perch above
a spitting neon proclamation
of FRESH EGGS and COLD BEER.
But who could help fidgeting
when coming up in those days meant
taking what was there and shaping it
by the ugly crease of your hands
passed down from the silver man
whose face I massaged while eyeing
the Dugout Rumble bubble gum
and too-sugared whips of Cow Tails,
knowing my lot was too little?
In that town and time we spat names
like they were ridged in copper: Sugar Bear, Bud,
Golds, and Pony, who knew
when to close shop and when the coast was at its clearest,
all from the throne of his Mongoose out front.
And I was just another, under the cool apathy
of the grocery fluorescents, waiting for a change,
counting on it.

Weird Diamonds

It happened there: cluttered by notes from the liner
and our unshapely youth, in your basement
as we sat around twin speakers like a campfire,

picking through the distortion and grueling bellows
spun wild from the black circle that we found
in your parents' collection and set gently

down under the crooked arm. We noted the pierce
and low thrum of blood in our palms
as we smacked them across our legs and torsos

on through the last blast of wood on tom and across
the silent scape that shifts into the strangest cry we'd heard yet,
a noise unfurled spat by awkward spat into a passable accordion

and that same voice from before, showing us
two ways to make a shining thing out of pure plain grit.

Coyote *in Adolescentia*

You shared all the soldiers in your collection. The infantrymen
crouched in their vigilance, their helmets sleek, their hands

expectant on the trigger of a rifle, a rocket launcher, a humpbacked
radio. I noticed in your hands small mutations when I took one

into the other room. At that age, there are two types of fear:
of lost trinkets and of the acceptance of such.

Little brother. Little bumble of pent aggravation. I caught you
mid-riot, aiming your boyhood at our encampment of figurines,

raining upon them as a way to stay young, in outright refusal
to use "the bad bathroom." Afterward, you shared a smile

amid the washing of plastic men. What a handful you became.
    Little crack
of ass toward the video camera because you thought it was funny.

Little continuing to moon
because I laughed along.

Dispatch from Here ('99)

Shaken to life and set shivering in the early untempered hours,
those caught between the webby glower of stars
and their slow-death-by-daylight, he wakes me,
while I stitch my aim like a hook
into the side of a dream that broke with the waking:
rope bridge, burlap full of rubies, careful work of a henchman's torch
gnawing at the last tether…

I dress in layers, knowing the chill of his van en route
and how long until the sun. First there are people to meet,
squat warehousers steering lifts and dollies, loading us up
with newspapers, one for each number on our list.
I roll while he drives, his hands tight on the leather wheel,
his gloves snug and faultlined, threatening to quake
as he pilots our way through the dormant streets.

And so the morning slowburns into a tentative orange peering
from behind the rooftops. All the while my hands make telescopes
out of newsprint, inky traces of story settling in the ridges of my fingers,
a shadow-me smeared across each surface I touch, spectral traces

marking my stake in our little house by the potbellied septics,
which shine like wet boulders in the new morning light
as neighbors slink home or away, to or from their posts or beds
or dark business among the cul-de-sacs.
By the morning's end and the last tossed paper,

he is red-eyed, proud, his rattle-along days pausing to scrape a paycheck
and some gasoline, to feed these stray children and the woman he's
    taken to,
to cull me from sleep again tomorrow, my hands still smoky,
to roll my telescopes again, turn by turn, we heralds
delivering what's needed for the long day to come.

Me and Coyote's Last Stand

Back to back summers you and I were sent to the garage
to congratulate the sky on a hard-earned 108°
and greet the heavy flies that came with it,

their thick static droning in our ears. By smallness
they came through slit screen doors
like hands into cool water. They made a home
of our home, gluing rice-grain eggs
along the innards of our trash cans until

they split into pale larvae, a bloodline
so pervasive our unborn children yet twitch
to swat them away.

Garage war of shadows and humidity. Of dust-ash
smeared hard across our foreheads.
We were the first line, armed to sweaty teeth
with wooden signposts you ripped from
their mundane FOR SALE lives. You knew

the sharp edge and angle, the just-right pressure
for each maggot's belly, stopping the crawl dead.
Those days our garage rang out with the sharp slap and stab
of cheap wood on concrete. From the street

we looked like pretend apes, smacking sticks on the ground
in a primal frustration, in want of a better way—
fire.

Strike a Match, Blacken

the punk's head
        launch a fiery clap into the sky
and gawk at the burst of chlorides and salt

        Today is July
and tomorrow is, and tonight…
        Brave boy with fire:
let the wind blow the bawl and cackle
        of friends down from your roof
as we stabilize our fifty
        dollar PALM TREE FINALE in the alleyway

It's a night for ruins
        so why not here? Why not
a severed finger for a story in the morning?
        You have your light and I
cling to it as we crouch to ignite
        a chemical riot in the dark
above us, our audience
        cheering and indiscernible
as the four, three, two,
        run, one…

Poem for A.'s Incisor

Tweezer careful,
I pluck it from her palm.

It's longer than expected, slick
and vibrating raw.

With the wash rag over her mouth
reddening in thick waves, I drop

the calcified sisterpiece
into a glass of water

and bring it to the table,
the space between her teeth groaning

behind the dampened cloth.
My father, my mother,

they dab the swollen pit
of her mouth in a sort of frantic

slowness hemmed in emergency.
Their eyes unblinking, wide

under the bulbous kitchen lights,
the tooth's wet sheen.

Muscles and blood tremor
in my sister's face

at the ache of something
fearsome and alive

and absent from the ridge of her mouth,
at the danger of inventing

a new shape for herself
mid-leap on the black trampoline.

Her head thrown forward. Her knee,
a hammer. She cut the air

like a blade, a helicopter
seed ground-bound,

eager for the wind's instruction
and wondrous everafter.

Rising Action

The summer the eagles came. A convocation of snowcapped symbols barking from the tips of telephone poles. Loud and mobile, hooded in white feathers. Of them all, that season was marked most by noise and eerie bursts of shadow on the sidewalks. I left the house only to drag broom teeth across the pavement out front, only when told. My father's space in our basement, for the first time, hushed. Like the best of us, they were quiet only after dark. I was growing in ways not unknown. I had more hunger. I was irritated and in love with the girls who seemed to slit their eyes, winking. Every morning meant early-screaming. My hands remained my hands.

About the Bird

I said nothing,
no mention of the cold rain pimpling
her puddle bath like so many fingers
massaging the skin
of our anniversary balloon.
It was quiet, Tuesday, the clouds slid
gray into gray as the bird
filed her feathers tight as scales
and plashed her head in the water
then shook off the droplets, plashed and shook,
all to make herself believe,
I believed, that the body is no hard shape,
is something that can be molded
and smoothed and pinched flat
into the shining swerve of a body in flight,
above or below the surface,
where doesn't matter so long as it's in
what sharpened peeking sunlight
there is to be had.

On Refraction

I'm doing it again, wrongly claiming fog when I can't see beyond the yard
for the myopic growths in this, my very head. And when I only see the stretch

of yard and nothing farther and cite fogishness as cause, that is me unawakened
to my own body, the faulty organs nestled just behind their lids, their miscalculated

interpreting of *this lone fencepost* or *mangled rot of shed wall*. A casual blur I often forget
to correct in the morning's clumsy waking, pried open by what I assume is

branch after branch of what I assume are trees in the corner of the yard.
But this short sight has been good to me. It's taught me better the tassels of grass

nearer the house, the way unclarity binds them in a single, muted smear
the farther out I cast my sight; and how that smear conveys only motion or no-motion,

brown smudge tearing across the garden as presumed rabbit,
brown smudge tearing nowhere as presumed stump;

and the narrow figure, wavering out of the horizon, undeterred,
black and sharp pink bound blurry, presumably you,

trekking in from the humidity and an eight mile run, bringing with you
the sweat and scorch of waspish summer.

You are grown out of distance and its dissolution;
defined by the sweep of your stride, closer now

than in all of my morning with this unanswerable company,
punctuation dissolving into its burrows, skipping to clear a way

for you, now bloomed, your face glistening with labor,
the pink of your shirt shining hot, and the clarification

of your place in this singular blurscape,
kiss by kiss by kiss.

In the Park with False Ruins

settled pool deep and spitting;
                the park with the shrine

of composers' heads
                horseshoeing a gazebo

of tinsel and balloons,
                it was a relief to find

myself away from the party,
                amongst the birches

with bark gray and fast grayer
                in its peely season.

I chose them over handclaps,
                over sugar-stuck candles.

The cold slinking
                back to its cavern

mottled in shadow,
                like the patches so brown

spilled along
                the slope of a giraffe.

Theory of the Wild

Cloud-caked sky from here to horizon,
formless gray swirls like soft gears

malleable in the machinery of night,
a massive slow-flood of steel and thunder.

From my stoop it's clear the Chinese Lantern Festival
diverts the neighborhood's usual rhythm

—the sputtered growl of passing subwoofers,
the distant *poppop* of desperation, of circumstance—

as visitors cast wonder like offerings
at the massive feet of two porcelain dragons:

towering, gnashing, blood-hungry
(according to their design)

and sheathed in painted flatware, homage
to those Han artisans who gave shape

to the monsters, maybe for fear of their realness,
tales traded of talons and fire-breath razing a distant village

in the dark swath of night; maybe for fear
of no real thing at all, the squeeze of such notions

on the mind's fibrous structures. And though
these clouds are real, their sound immense as history,

the festival wages on into the makings of a key-cold night,
the people clamping to their surprise

as the dragons advance and retreat,
advance and retreat, like dancers

on a watery stage, the pattern rehearsed
until seamless as weather.

In the Heaving of a Static Stampede

the terrible lean-and-sway of the festival's giant
mechanical dragons—the size of them corrosive
to the sight, as space's black corrodes faint stars—

the garden drew tight its walkways and I
caught, in the palms of my eyes, a gash
of light flickering like an insect

from their many burial-tight plates and teacups
      —a spackled skin of armor—

causing me to look down from commotion and finally take note
of the pond's limp moss obstructing ripples
in the dragons' thunderous swagger.

Traces

We could talk of noise under the sheets like sand
shifting in an open jar. Of this hot oval,

red on my forearm. Of the wrinkled
body-length span of bed sheet. There are

so many things that dissolve. More so,
there is a table and what remains

of an orange, its peel shattered
across the face of a glass plate.

Year of the Goat

It doesn't matter,
the sheet metal thunder
rattling house and body,

shaking us rung by rung clear
out of our separate storms.

You are one thing
at the doorway,
another once fully entered,

boarded as the windows
we shy away from.

And me? I am battered
and bashing at the threshold,
newly antlered, my head

wired with bone and
the seeds of a flame

we thought hushed
when those loud winds boiled
over the edge of town.

The new year has risen.
Let's forgive ourselves

the old ways of caring,
the bodily zodiac
of furtive glances,

breath marking the skin
like steam.

Hands in their
separate wringings.
However the gray

ribbon of fortune falls,
however the days

crumple into dusk,
there will still be
shelter and arms

and the cool crust
of the earth below

as we lay and name
each dart of lightning
that slips into the house
like the stray that it is.

Black Tern

In many ways, we are lucky.
We have our strength, the heft of our bodies
rising each morning. A cellar of vegetables
strangely magnified in their cap-locked vinegar.
Our house on the most imposing hill.

And when that dark clutch of birds rested at the lake
to feed on what grounded creatures remain,
we had an ornithologist to tell us
"no, not crows" and "maybe terns,
black terns due elsewhere," his binoculars peekish
between the boarded windows.
And so, we wince at the blue crash of sky on grass,
the peppering of specks by the water,
and tally our luck again from the beginning.

Grip and Hammer

The jagged grin of a can
chiseled gaping by hammer
and my sure grasp; a nail
cut like red coral into my hand
and punctured the aluminum to soil
a sticky hideaway for sliced
mandarin oranges. This is the way

I betray you. In sweetness, in tang,
in the glint of clouded syrup
on a tip or two of my fingers
—all clear thought of you shuffled under
in the deck of my clamorous body.

I beat a nail into this penultimate can
for fear of the grrrring outside world,
to stave off the dogs beneath my skin,
their eyes yellow as the sky
in the middle of the city's last good night.

The wreckage made, the sugars dried
and mawkish, I turn to face the daylight
spidering through the planks and grime
that cover our windows. Far off,

a revving takes stage in a story unlike
the one we've drafted here, in this lone shed.
Something I still think true,
the hammer firm in my grip.

Louder, nearer, it calls
for our attention. I only hope
you don't wake too soon.

No Image

What perverse joy
to drive along the interstate

and see a van stalled in the margin
and behind that, and within, the image of fire

radiating blurred waves
only to learn, the closer we get,

that there is no image
but real fire

transforming the dry grass,
the manicured upholstery

in a way I could
never wholly mimic.

Lookaftering

You wake and find the pantry converted,
each label about-faced,
then the utensils, swaying
when the window is locked.
Do not be afraid.
See. Now I tighten the drawer knob
that flirts with detachment.
Cut through yesterday
on the calendar with a slice
of dark ink.
These are the things
you come to each morning.
In life, from room to room,
always the picture frames
need adjusting, the soap refilling.
Do not be afraid.
Count the house keys
in the dish where you left them.
Count the reserve light bulbs
from which one is still missing,
its empty slot stark as the space
knocked into our neighbor's front teeth
at the glint of the new year.
The slat gone from his fence.
This half-emptied closet,
my shirts wrapped in black plastic.
Look at the pathway leading to the entry
door that is now all yours.
Eight stones total, four split
and yawning, one monogrammed,
the arc of letters tangled and black
as eels moving over dry land.
This waits to fill my tomorrow
and the days after. Rocks
and their broken cousins;

rocks sleeping in the yard
among the motion of the living.
Do not be afraid.
The matches are where you left them.

Ray **Holmes** received his MFA in poetry at the University of Missouri-St. Louis, where he was twice awarded 2nd place in the program's James Russell Grant Poetry Contest. His writing has appeared in such journals as *Architrave Press, Chariton Review, Dialogist, Fjords, Midwestern Gothic, Thin Air*, and others. He served as adjunct faculty for community colleges and an assistant editor for local literary journals before finding his home as a high school educator. He currently lives in St. Louis, Missouri, with his wife and their three rescue pets. [Instagram @schmayschmolmes]

www.ingramcontent.com/pod-product-compliance
Lightning Source LLC
LaVergne TN
LVHW041556070426
835507LV00011B/1108